CANADA'S
DINOSAURS

Text by Chelsea Donaldson
Illustrations by John Bindon

Scholastic Canada Ltd.

Toronto New York London Auckland Sydney
Mexico City New Delhi Hong Kong Buenos Aires

Scholastic Canada Ltd.
604 King Street West, Toronto, Ontario M5V 1E1

Scholastic Inc.
557 Broadway, New York, NY 10012, USA

Scholastic Australia Pty Limited
PO Box 579, Gosford, NSW 2250, Australia

Scholastic New Zealand Limited
Private Bag 94407, Greenmount, Auckland, New Zealand

Scholastic Children's Books
Euston House, 24 Eversholt Street, London NW1 1DB, UK

Every reasonable effort has been made to trace the ownership of copyright materials used in the text.
The publisher would be pleased to know of any errors or omissions.

Visual Credits
PHOTO CREDITS: p. 3: © Peabody Museum of Natural History, Yale University, New Haven, Connecticut,
USA; pp. 11, 23 (centre inset), 25, 26, 36: Photo courtesy of the Royal Tyrrell Museum, Drumheller,
Alberta; pp. 20, 21: Photo by Jim Page/Courtesy of the North Carolina Museum of Natural Sciences; p. 23
(top right): Stephen Ausmus/United States Dept. of Agriculture (USDA), Agricultural Research Service;
p. 23 (top left): Carla Stanley/United States Fish and Wildlife Service (USFWS); p. 24: Image #17808/
American Museum of Natural History Library; p. 35: © Charles Helm; p. 41: Used with permission
of the University of California Museum of Paleontology (UCMP)/photo by David K. Smith
ILLUSTRATION CREDITS: Illustrations (all) © John D. Bindon, 2009

Developed and Produced by Focus Strategic Communications Inc.
Project Management and Editorial: Adrianna Edwards
Editorial and Production Assisting: Layla Moola
Design and Layout: Valentino Sanna
Illustrations: John Bindon
Photo Research: Elizabeth Kelly

Special thanks to Hall Train of Hall Train Studios for his expertise.

Library and Archives Canada Cataloguing in Publication
Donaldson, Chelsea, 1959–
Canada's dinosaurs / by Chelsea Donaldson ; illustrated by John Bindon.
(Canada close up)
ISBN 978-0-545-98972-5
1. Dinosaurs — Canada — Juvenile literature.
I. Bindon, John II. Title. III. Series: Canada close up (Toronto, Ont.)
QE861.5.D68 2009   j567.90971   C2009-901793-8

6 5 4 3 2 1   Printed in Canada   09 10 11 12 13

Mixed Sources
Product group from well-managed
forests and other controlled sources
www.fsc.org Cert no. SGS-COC-003098
© 1996 Forest Stewardship Council
FSC

TABLE OF CONTENTS

Canada's Dinosaurs

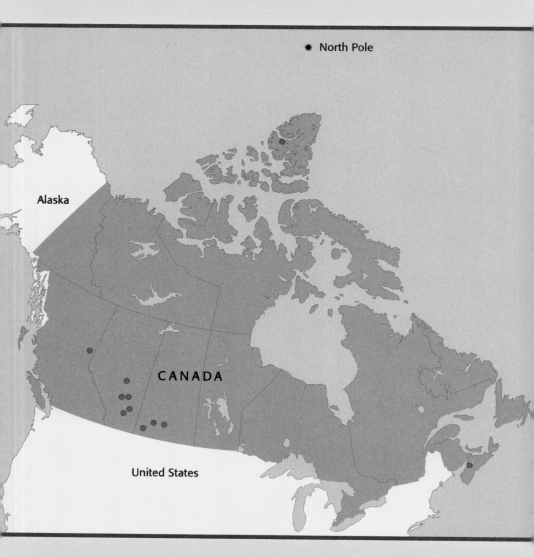

North Pole

Alaska

CANADA

United States

● Canada's Dinosaurs — Dig Sites

Canada

United States

Welcome to Prehistoric Canada!

For about 200 million years, dinosaurs were among the biggest, fiercest creatures on Earth. Then, about 65 million years ago, they disappeared. What happened? No one knows for sure.

We know dinosaurs once lived on Earth because we have found their bones. Over time, minerals filled the bones and they became rocklike. These "rocks" are called fossils. Fossils can also come from impressions in the ground, made by things like footprints, skin or poop.

Although dinosaurs lived all over the world, some spots are better for finding fossils. In Canada, Alberta has the most dinosaur bones. In fact, it is one of the best places in the world to hunt for dinosaurs! Dinosaur remains have also been found in British Columbia, Nova Scotia, Nunavut and Saskatchewan. Let's find out more about Canada's dreadful dinos!

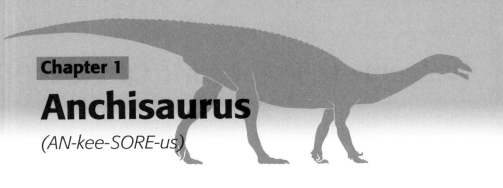

Chapter 1

Anchisaurus
(AN-kee-SORE-us)

Anchisaurus bones were the first dinosaur fossils found in North America. In 1818, no one knew about dinosaurs. They figured the strange bones were from ancient humans.

How could anyone mistake a dinosaur for a human? Well, for one thing, the bones were very old and broken up. For another, Anchisaurus was only about the size of a small pony, or a very large human.

Besides, if you didn't already know that dinosaurs existed, how could you possibly dream them up?

Since then, we've learned more about Anchisaurus. For example, we know it was one of the earliest dinosaurs. It lived 195 million years ago.

Back then, Earth had just one giant continent. Later, it broke apart and the pieces drifted off to form the continents we know today. That explains why Anchisaurus fossils have been found in places as far apart as Nova Scotia and South Africa. They used to be right next door to each other!

Anchisaurus bones

We also know that Anchisaurus was probably one of the first prosauropods (pro-SAW-ro-pods). Prosauropods were plant-eating dinos with long necks, small heads, short forelimbs and very large thumb claws. Anchisaurus was one of the smallest of this group.

The teeth of Anchisaurus were small and spoon-shaped, good for tearing off plants. It had a big belly to help it digest tough, stringy vegetation. It is possible that it ate meat as well, but we don't know for sure.

Most of the time, Anchisaurus probably moved slowly on all fours, keeping its head close to the ground. But when danger threatened, it may have been able to lift up on its hind legs and run. There's nothing like a giant meat-eating lizard chasing after you to keep you on your toes!

Chapter 2

Tyrannosaurus Rex

(ty-RAN-o-SORE-us RECKS)

THUMP . . . THUMP . . . THUMP.

Can't you just hear the heart-stopping footsteps of this massive dinosaur? Watch out — it's Tyrannosaurus rex!

T. rex isn't the largest dinosaur ever found, but it is definitely one of the most famous — and the most terrifying! In fact, its name means "king of the terrible lizards."

Its head was about as big as you are! It also had up to 60 sharp, pointy teeth, each one about as tall as this page. Those teeth sat in a hinged jaw that could open *very* wide — so wide that an adult human would have slid down its throat nice and easy! (Luckily, no humans were around when T. rex ruled the Earth.)

Its jaw and neck muscles were so strong, it could have picked up a cow — if it could have found one! T. rex had no trouble crunching through bones.

As with most dinos, there is still a lot we don't know about Tyrannosaurus. For one thing, how did it get its food? Some scientists think it was a hunter. They point to its strong neck and jaws, which could have held on tightly to a struggling animal. But others suggest that T. rex was a scavenger. Scavengers eat the remains of creatures caught by other animals.

Perhaps both groups are right. Perhaps these giant creatures hunted *and* scavenged, grabbing food any way they could.

We also don't know much about young Tyrannosaurus. So far, only a few fossils of T. rex babies have been found. One was from a dinosaur that was around two years old when it died and about the size of a large dog. It had teeth shaped for biting into flesh. It's likely that a young T. rex hunted small prey on its own. It was very well adapted for hunting because it was quick and small but still had a big bite!

Chapter 3

Parasaurolophus

(PAR-a-sore-OL-o-fus)

Parasaurolophus is one of the oddest-looking dinos you'll ever see. What on earth is that long thing sticking out of the back of its head? It looks a bit like an elephant's trunk that got put on backwards.

Parasaurolophus belongs to a group of dinosaurs called the duckbills. Many duckbill dinos had odd-shaped heads, with bony crests of various shapes and sizes. But none had crests quite as big as this.

Duckbills were one of the last dinosaur groups to appear. They first showed up around 100 million years ago. They are called duckbills because they had hard, flat, beak-like mouths with no teeth in front — a bit like those of ducks.

Parasaurolophus's beak acted like a weed whacker for cutting off tough plant stems. Then specially shaped teeth in the side of the mouth went to work, grinding and chopping up the hard, stringy food.

So that explains the beak. But what was that head crest for? For many years, scientists didn't really know. They wondered if maybe the long bony head gear was designed like a snorkel, for breathing underwater. Others suggested the long horn helped the duckbill to smell. A good sense of smell would have given them early warning of predators.

Today, some researchers believe the crest acted like a musical instrument. The dino could blow air through the hollow tubes to produce a mating call or to warn other dinos of danger.

One group of researchers has even managed to recreate what Parasaurolophus might have sounded like. They think the call would have been a bit like a trombone, or maybe a foghorn. Either way, it must have made the prehistoric forests very noisy places!

Chapter 4

Lambeosaurus

(LAM-bee-o-SORE-us)

Here's another creature with a strange head. This one looks like it's got a small hatchet buried under its skin! If you guessed that this is another duckbill dino like Parasaurolophus, you're right.

Lambeosaurus is named after Lawrence Lambe, a famous Canadian dino researcher. Back in 1898, he found the first evidence of these dinosaurs, at a place called Berry Creek, in Alberta. Now duckbills like Lambeosaurus are among the most common types of dinosaur fossils found in Canada.

Lambeosaurus is the largest duckbill
dinosaur discovered so far. From its beak
to its tail, it measured about 15 metres.
That's about the width of a basketball
court. It could walk on two legs, or drop
down on all fours to reach low-lying plants.
Although Lambeosaurus was big, it was
probably a fast runner. It had to be — to stay
out of the way of predators like T. rex!

Another way that Lambeosauruses protected themselves was by sticking close to each other. Large herds of these giants would graze together, like sheep or deer do today. If a predator was sighted, they would warn their neighbours by bellowing, honking or bleating.

Lambeosaurus probably also used its call, along with its crest, to attract a mate. Some researchers think the crest may have been covered in brightly coloured skin, like a rooster's comb.

We don't know much about how Lambeosauruses cared for their young, but we do have some clues from another type of duckbill dinosaur — Maiasaurus (MY-a-SORE-us). Maiasauruses built lots of nests in one area. That way, they could take turns protecting the eggs and covering them with plants to keep them warm. The adults may have continued to look after the babies after they hatched — just like a duckbill daycare centre!

Did Lambeosaurus and other duckbills do the same? It's quite possible, but we don't really know.

Chapter 5

Thescelosaurus

(THES-ke-lo-SORE-us)

The full name of this plant-eater is Thescelosaurus neglectus, which means "marvelous reptile, forgotten or overlooked." It earned its name because the first fossils found were left in a crate for more than 20 years. It wasn't until 1913 that researchers even gave it a name!

Since then, remains of Thescelosaurus have been found in Saskatchewan, Alberta and in several places in the United States.

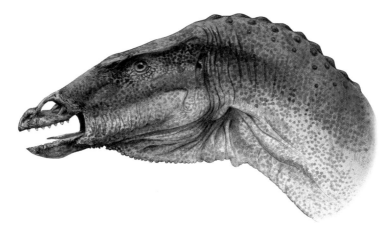

Thescelosaurus was medium sized for a dinosaur
— about four metres long. It stood less than a
metre tall, with round scales of different sizes
all over its body. It had a small, hard beak, with
teeth on either side of its mouth. These would
have helped it to grind up plants and leaves.

Fossilized heart

Thescelosaurus skeleton

Thescelosaurus may have started out as a forgotten dino, but today, it's getting lots of attention. In 1993, researchers uncovered a well-preserved Thescelosaurus skeleton in North America. Inside the ribcage they found a hard rock that some experts think is a fossilized heart!

If it is, in fact, a dino heart, it's the first example of one ever uncovered. Usually, soft parts of the body like heart, lungs and skin disappear over time, leaving only the hard bits, like bone.

The skeleton is so important, it has been given its own nickname — Willo. Its "heart" has been examined by doctors, fossil experts and many others. They were surprised to find that it was more like a human or bird heart than a lizard heart. If this is true, it could make us rethink a lot of what we thought we knew about dinosaurs.

Pretty amazing for a medium-sized, forgotten lizard!

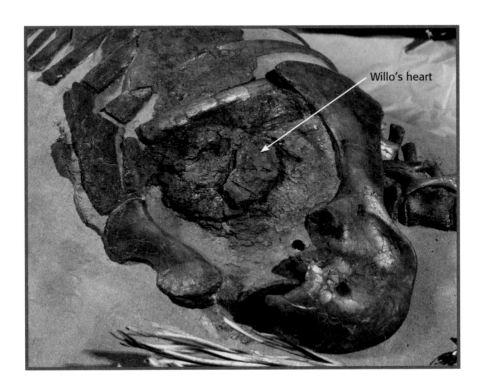

Willo's heart

Chapter 6

Dromaeosaurus

(DRO-me-o-SORE-us)

Here's something that may surprise you: dinosaurs never really became extinct. In fact, you probably see real, living dino descendants just about every day. Think of that sparrow sitting outside your window . . . or the chicken you had for supper last night . . . or the ostrich you saw at the zoo. All of these are modern-day cousins of the dinosaurs.

One dinosaur that shares some features with
some modern birds, like chickens or sparrows,
is Dromaeosaurus. Dromaeosaurus was about the
size of a wolf. That's big for a bird, but small for
a dinosaur. Some of its bones were hollow like
bird bones are. It's even likely that it was covered
with feathers. But since feathers don't usually get
preserved in fossils, we don't really know.

Even if Dromaeosaurus *was* feathered,
it probably didn't actually fly. The feathers
were likely used for warmth.

The first dromaeosaur fossils were discovered near the Red Deer River in Alberta. They were dug up by a fossil hunter called Barnum Brown. He and his friend William Diller Matthew called the fossil Dromaeosaurus albertensis, meaning "running lizard of Alberta." Since then, fossils that are similar to Dromaeosaurus have been found in other places. Scientists group them all under the name dromaeosaurs.

Dromaeosaurs were definitely meat-eaters. They had strong pointy teeth that could tear through flesh easily. Their front limbs had sharp claws.

On their back legs they had "sickle claws" that stood upright. They likely used their claws to rip open their prey.

And let's not forget their wicked kick. Dromaeosaurs had special leg muscles to help them pack a real punch. In addition to all that, they were fast — really fast. Their light bones and small size made it easy for them to catch their prey.

Who would have thought that chickens and chickadees had such scary ancestors!

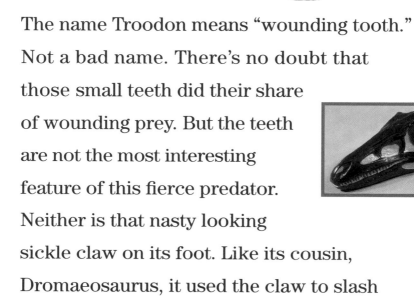

Chapter 7
Troodon
(TRO-o-don)

The name Troodon means "wounding tooth."
Not a bad name. There's no doubt that
those small teeth did their share
of wounding prey. But the teeth
are not the most interesting
feature of this fierce predator.
Neither is that nasty looking
sickle claw on its foot. Like its cousin,
Dromaeosaurus, it used the claw to slash
at the hide of other animals.

Because Troodon was small and light like other raptor-type dinosaurs, it could run very fast and change direction easily. It had long forelimbs, which could reach out and grab hold of things. It may even have had feathers (although it couldn't fly).

But these still aren't its most interesting features. There's something else that makes Troodon special.

Its brain.

For its size, Troodon may have had a bigger brain than any other dinosaur. That probably makes it the cleverest dinosaur ever — bad news for the small animals like frogs, lizards and perhaps birds that it preyed on.

Brainpower may have allowed Troodon to develop a new way of hunting. In addition to tracking down small prey on its own, Troodons may have hunted together in packs — much like wolves or coyotes do. That would have allowed them to capture much larger prey, such as young Parasaurolophuses.

Of course, even the smartest dinosaurs were not nearly as intelligent as humans — or even most animals of today. But for its time, Troodon was one smart cookie!

Troodon may have been a scary predator, but it was also a caring parent. Several Troodon nests have been found, some with more than 20 eggs in them, each about the size of a melon. Scientists think a group of females may have shared the same nest. It's even possible that male Troodons helped out with the nesting duties. No doubt the moms were tired after laying all those giant eggs!

Chapter 8
Ornithomimus
(OR-nith-o-MY-muss)

In 1890, fossil hunter Othniel Marsh was studying a few small bones from a new type of dinosaur. He noticed that the foot bone looked a bit like that of a modern-day bird. He called the creature Ornithomimus, which means "bird-mimic."

The name turned out to be quite accurate. Later, when researchers in Alberta found an almost complete skeleton of an Ornithomimus, it became clear that this was a very bird-like dinosaur. It was like an ostrich with arms!

Ostriches are not actually related to
Ornithomimus, but they do share a lot of the
same features. They both have long, thin necks,
slender heads, big eyes and toothless beaks.
And look at those long spindly legs. Don't they
look like they would be good for running?

Of course, there are differences as well.
Ornithomimus had two strong hands, which it
may have used to pull down branches. It also had
a long tail to help balance out its body.

Remember that we said those legs looked like they would be good for running? Well, they were. Ornithomimus was probably one of the fastest dinosaurs of all time. This would have come in handy when T. rex came calling.

When Ornithomimus ran, it probably stuck its neck forward in the shape of an S, like an ostrich does. Experts say it was at least as fast as an ostrich, which can travel up to 80 kilometres per hour!

There are still some mysteries about Ornithomimus. For example, did it have scales or feathers? Many dinosaur specialists think Ornithomimus was actually covered in a soft, fluffy layer of fuzz, like the down on a baby chick.

Scientists would also like to know what an Ornithomimus supper looked like. Some think it would include only plants. But many experts agree that Ornithomimus ate just about anything — plants, roots and seeds as well as small frogs, worms and bugs. YUM!

Chapter 9

Ankylosaurus

(AN-kee-lo-SORE-us)

It's not always the experts who make big dinosaur discoveries. Sometimes, ordinary people come across important fossils and have the imagination to recognize what they have found.

That's what happened in the summer of 2000, near Tumbler Ridge, British Columbia. Eleven-year-old Mark Turner and nine-year-old Daniel Helm were floating down a creek when they noticed some dents in the rocks along the shore. When they looked more closely, they knew right away what they had found — dinosaur tracks!

Mark and Daniel rubbed white powder into the tracks so they could see them more clearly. They asked a fossil expert to check out the strange markings. It turns out Mark and Daniel were right. The prints were made by an Ankylosaurus, or armoured dinosaur.

So far, no one has found a complete fossil skeleton of Ankylosaurus. But we know that it was one of the biggest of the armoured dinosaurs. It was covered from its head to its tail in bony plates and spikes. It looked like a prehistoric battle tank. Even its eyelids were armour plated!

Ankylosaurus weighed up to four tonnes and was probably about as wide and long as a large elephant with its trunk sticking out. But, at only about 1.5 metres tall, it was much shorter. That's short enough that if you met one, you could climb up for a ride — if you dared!

Of course, you would have to watch out for the tail club, a bony knob about the size of a big beach ball. One swipe from that club was enough to break the leg of a Tyrannosaurus. So imagine what it might do to an unwanted passenger.

Generally speaking, though, Ankylosaurus probably just wanted to be left alone to munch on leaves and plants. It may have used its mighty club only to knock fruit down from the branches of trees — or when it had to defend itself.

That wasn't all that often, because the only way a predator could get past all that armour was to flip Ankylosaurus over onto its unprotected belly. But Ankylosaurus was so wide and so low to the ground, even giants like Tyrannosaurus couldn't have made it roll over!

Chapter 10

Triceratops

(tri-SERRA-tops)

One of the last groups of dinosaurs to appear was the ceratopsians (ser-a-TOP-see-uns), or horned dinosaurs. These big, tough-looking plant-eaters roamed the woodlands and swamps of Saskatchewan and Alberta for millions of years. There were many different types of horned dinos. The very last to develop was also the biggest . . .

. . . TRICERATOPS!

Most ceratopsians had two features that
were hard to miss. The first was their horns.
Triceratops had two horns above its eyes
that were as long as hockey sticks, and a
shorter one on its nose.

The second feature of ceratopsians was
the "frill" around their necks. It looked like the
shoulder pads that football players wear. In most
ceratopsians, the frill was actually too fragile
to be helpful as defence. But Triceratops's frill
was solid bone. One look at that great shield
and those horns was probably enough to
scare most predators.

We don't really know what the frill looked
like when it was covered in skin. Perhaps
it was brightly coloured to attract a mate.
Or maybe it changed colours depending on
the animal's mood. Some lizards today can
change colour like that.

Groups of Triceratops bones have been found
in the same area, so families may have stayed
together. Or perhaps they migrated as a group.
It's also possible they lived alone and the bones
just got moved together over time.

Scientists used to think there were many kinds of Triceratops, each with a slightly different frill and different horns. Slowly, they started to realize that there were actually only a few kinds. Most of the differences had to do with how old the Triceratopses were when they died.

A young Triceratops skull looks quite different from that of its parents. For one thing, its horns started out as little lumps and grew to their full

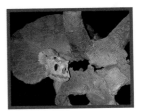

Baby and adult Triceratops skulls

length only as an adult. The shape of its face was different, too, and the frill was much smaller. You can see why scientists might be confused.

Dino Fact File

Now you've read about 10 of Canada's many dinosaurs. Which one is your favourite? You can use the chart below to check out some important facts about each dinosaur or to compare one dino to another.

Name	Type	Where in Canada?
Dromaeosaurus	Raptor	Alberta
Troodon	Raptor	Alberta
Anchisaurus	Prosauropod	Nova Scotia
Thescelosaurus	Bird-footed	Alberta, Saskatchewan
Ornithomimus	Ostrich	Alberta
Ankylosaurus	Armoured	Alberta, British Columbia
Triceratops	Horned	Alberta, Saskatchewan
Parasaurolophus	Duck-billed	Alberta
Tyrannosaurus rex	Tyrannosaur	Alberta, Saskatchewan
Lambeosaurus	Duck-billed	Alberta, Nunavut

How Long?	How Heavy?	Diet
1.7 m	25 kg	Meat
2 m	25 kg	Meat
2.5 m	35 kg	Plants
3.5–4 m	300 kg	Plants
4–6 m	130–160 kg	Plants and meat
7–10 m	3-4 tonnes	Plants
9 m	5-8 tonnes	Plants
12 m	3 tonnes	Plants
12 m	6 tonnes	Meat
9–15 m	5–6 tonnes	Plants

The last big dinosaurs disappeared quite suddenly about 65 million years ago. What could have killed off so many creatures in such a short amount of time? Some scientists think a giant piece of space rock hit the Earth. It sent up a huge cloud of dust that blocked out the sun. Without sunlight, nothing could grow, and the dinosaurs starved.

Now that you're on your way to becoming a dinosaur expert, maybe someday you'll be the person to figure out what happened to them!

Big or small, scaly or feathered, Canada's dinosaurs are waiting to be discovered!